A COLLECTION OF EROTIC VISIONS

COREEN YAMA

Copyright © 2024 by Coreen Yama.

All rights reserved. No part of this publication may be reproduced, distributed, or transmitted in any form or by any means, including photocopying, recording, or other electronic or mechanical methods, without the written consent of the publisher. The only exceptions are for brief quotations included in critical reviews and other noncommercial uses permitted by copyright law.

MILTON & HUGO L.L.C.
4407 Park Ave., Suite 5
Union City, NJ 07087, USA

Website: *www.miltonandhugo.com*
Hotline: *1- 888-778-0033*
Email: *info@miltonandhugo.com*

Ordering Information:
Quantity sales. Special discounts are granted to corporations, associations, and other organizations. For more information on these discounts, please reach out to the publisher using the contact information provided above.

Library of Congress Control Number:	2024910631
ISBN-13: 979-8-89285-115-2	[Paperback Edition]
979-8-89285-114-5	[Digital Edition]

Rev. date: 05/02/2024

Wet Dreams

❖❖❖

I arise to see you sleeping exposing that next to me you are standing at attention. I hear the rhythm of your breathing as you sleep soundly. I start to caress my lush breasts, grabbing them firmly, pinching and twisting them, making my nipples hard. Knowing you are hard and I can play with you really turns me on. I moan to see if you wake up. You lie in quiet slumber, not disturbed. I smile to myself and move my hands to my pussy. I'm feeling the energy flow to my groin. My pulse is rising with each breath you take. I rub my pussy teasingly, playing with her until she responds. Her warm wetness and soft lips flood with juices. Now I want to seduce you.The rhythm of your breathing let me know you are unaware. I clasp your cock with both hands, and my mouth watering, I start to slurp on you, blowing and slurping all that you have. Your breath quickens. I continue this until my pussy is flowering. She is ready now; so I mount you, sliding you deeply into me, riding you like a cowgirl. I moan in euphoria. Your cock is so hard I move forward and backward, sliding my pussy over your pelvis. There I find it my sweet spot. Thrusting more vigorously now, I'm about to climax. I feel the pulsating in my pussy deep inside. Your breath is heavier now; your sleep is still very deep. I gasp and exhale as the gush of fluids rushes out of me. Startled, I wake up.

Time Away

⋙ ❖❖❖ ⋘

It's a hot breezy day. We are lying naked in the hotel room. You are caressing my thighs with your fingers and tongue. Arousing my senses from my daydreams, I'm fully into you. You begin licking my pussy from top to bottom. My juices are flowing. I give a little shake of delight. I feel the sensation of you pressing your tongue into me. Squealing, I grab you by the hair and pull you toward my flower. I feel the pressure of your fingers as they engulf my flower in circular motions. In walks the housekeeping maid, smiling expectantly. I'm wet and ready for what is going to happen. The maid immediately goes down on me with flicking tongue motions. You are stroking your hard shaft, observing curiously. I feel the heat in the room and the rush of sensual vibes. Lifting her lips up to my mouth, I passionately kiss her as I undo her uniform. She has a lush, firm body. We caress each other's breasts. You start sucking my supple nipples, and I'm stroking your firm cock. She moves down on me again. I feel the surge of energy pulsate through my body. I feel her hot tongue licking my pussy, sensually flicking and kissing as she goes. My pulse rises. I'm shaking in euphoria. I want to climax. I suck your shaft to keep from yelling. The energy in the room is magnetic; we are in utopia. Your shaft pulsates in my mouth. You are going to climax soon. She is moaning rhythmically as my hips quiver over her mouth. This is the moment I feel your cock thicken as the rush of your ejaculation slides down my throat and I climax. You taste so good. She sits up with my juices all over her face. We all collapse on the bed, breathing deeply to come back to earth.

Thrift Shopping

Shopping at the thrift store, enjoying the smell of the stale air and vintage clothes, I spot an old laptop. This is a real find for the price they are asking, so I decide to buy it. I take it home and charge it up, but then I notice burn marks on its edges. When I check through the computer, I find an old video file. Curious, I open it. Much to my surprise, I find a home movie of a man and woman engaging in erotic sexual play. He is tying her to the bed with ropes. He is wearing a mask with a zipper for the mouth and black slacks. She is wearing a blindfold and a white lace bra and thong. The room is very dark except for a dim light in the corner. You can barely make out her body lying on the bed. There is no sound, just her wiggling against the ropes. Her movements are subtle like she's enjoying herself. He is seducing her with a giant dildo, which he thrusts deeply into her. With each thrust, her hands grab at the ropes as she pulls away, thrashing her head side to side. I pause for a moment. This is deeply disturbing and yet mildly arousing. I'm startled with my emotions. I feel a surge of anger and excitement rush over my body. My heart is beating fast. *What will he do next?* I think. Then out of nowhere, he slaps her across the face. She wiggles and pulls away. Holding her by the chin, he licks her down the neck and to her bra. He grabs her breast and squeezes his hand tight. Then he rips off her bra, exposing firm round breasts with perky nipples. Still arousing me, I'm troubled by my feelings as I feel the perspiration forming on my brow. My pussy is wet. I want to turn it off, but I can't. These two people have me captive in their sinister world. I stop breathing for a moment—he is urinating on her. I close my eyes. *No more*, I think. Now he is pouring something over her. I see the match. I close the laptop, crying now as I realize she is me. I smell the match and feel the flame as it tinges my skin. *No more*, I think and release myself from the pain. Like a phoenix, I rise out of the ashes wiping away the tears, vowing never again to be submissive to a man.

Thoughts of You

⋙ ❖❖❖ ⋘

I'm at work thinking about you, your arousing physique. I'm daydreaming about kissing your firm, sensual lips. This arouses me. I feel the energy rush between my legs as I become warm and my nipples become erect. I hope my colleagues don't notice. I rush to the bathroom. I must play with myself. Your presence is so powerful over me. In the bathroom, I close and lock the door. Facing the mirror, I remove my top. My nipples are fully erect. I start caressing myself, first my breasts, squeezing tightly, pinching my nipples softly. I imagine you are here. I lick my lips to taste your mouth. The heat between my legs is making my pussy swell and wet. My juices are flowing! I put my hand up my skirt and feel the smooth, soft skin of my thighs. I move my fingers to my thong—it's wet and juicy! I moan loudly as I passionately caress my pussy. My senses are heightened as passion is taking over my body, causing energy to flow from the top of my head to my toes. My pulse is racing. A dewy sweat is forming on my skin, which conflicts with the coolness of the washroom. I want to climax! I imagine you kissing and licking me as I rub my clit the right way. I gasp erotically. I feel my lips quivering as the gushing happens between my legs. My warm, wet juices flow like water down my legs, soaking the floor. Tears of joy and fulfillment begin running down my face.

Tacos

⬥❖❖❖⬥

We are in Mexico, and we want to try authentic tacos. We go to a couple massages on the beach in the privacy of a tent. The ocean breeze is blowing. The sound of the waves splashing rhythmically against the sand is euphoric. The massage therapist lays us on our backs. Using sensual-smelling oils, she begins our massage. Starting at my shoulders, she rubs her hands down my front over my breasts and stops at my waist continually. This arouses both of us. She slowly moves her hands back to my now-erect supple nipples, caressing them seductively with gentle squeezing and pinching. This is turning you on as I can see your juices flowing from between your legs. I'm feeling sexy, and my juices are flowing as the energy rushes to my pussy. I want more as the heat becomes strong between my legs. She moves to the side of the massage table and begins massaging my inner thighs. With each breath I take, I feel all the tension leaving me. Slowly she moves closer to my pussy. My pulse rises. This is really happening to us. I know you are aroused too because I hear the moans coming from you as they massage your groin. Her very strong fingers are rubbing circular motions on my clit. I'm very wet and juicy. She slips a finger in. I moan with glee. Your masseuse is now sitting on your face as you fully enjoy sucking on her luscious pussy. I'm moaning loudly now as I observe you and her. The rubbing and fingers in me feels like ecstasy. I'm hearing everything, the ocean waves that slap against the sand. My senses are heightened. I smell the salty air. I want to climax as I feel the pulsing deep inside my pussy. I breathe in the salty air, and with a yelp, I release. My whole body is climaxing because I quiver and get shivers of energy flow through my body. I release to the euphoria and squirt. You sit up and say authentic tacos. We all laugh.

Roommate

❖❖❖

I answer an advertisement for a roommate. This handsome, strong man answers the door. He shows me the furnished bedroom that I will be staying in. I think it's perfect and agree to stay. Every night I masturbate to climax and relax to fall asleep. I fantasize about my roommate coming in and joining me. Leaving the door open, I hope that I can entice him to come in. I start up my vibrator. The rhythmic hum has me moaning enthusiastically as the vibrations massage my pussy. Out of the corner of my eye, I see a shadow coming along the hall and hear him quietly calling my name. My heart races as the shadow materializes as him. Smiling, he pushes the door open. He can see my pussy is extremely wet as she drips on the bedsheet. He comes toward me, his cock enlarged in his sweatpants. His masculine hands reach for my breasts and seductively caress them. I feel all my senses heighten. I smell his cologne mixed with his perspiration. I hear the humming of my vibrator. My nipples are erect as he begins sucking on them. I pull off his pants. I'm breathing heavy in deep long breaths. He bends me over the footboard and slowly, deeply thrusts his hard cock inside of me. My pussy is pulsing and swollen. On every thrust, I feel the euphoria of the moment. I climax with a gasp, my whole body quivering. I have to taste him. I spin around, and grasping his cock with both hands, I quickly start sucking and licking the head. He gasps now. I deep-throat him, slowly drawing up and down. He's moaning uncontrollably. He shoots down my throat, making me climax again, releasing my juices all over the bedsheets. I don't stop sucking him, and I lick the head of his cock, sending him into the shakes till he begs me to stop. As we rise, the bed is soaking with my essence and his perspiration. This is a good thing as we escape to his room to sleep.

Retail Shopping

❖❖❖

I walk into a retail shop to buy clothing. The manager sees I'm a fashion mess; and she starts asking questions about me—my likes, what I'm interested in, and stuff. We start chatting. Her smile is like sunshine to me. I can't get her out of my mind. I spend all I have to stay with her chatting. As I'm leaving, she hugs me tightly with her athletic body. She says, "Give me your number so I can call you for future promotions." Happiness fills my heart, and I give her my number. Later as I'm home opening my packages, the phone rings. It's her! She has a special offer for me. I'm to meet her at a bar, wearing the new clothes I bought. So l prepare excitedly. We arrive together. She hugs me passionately. We chat for a while, and I can't help but laugh. She has extremely attractive, supple breasts and perfect ass. I steal a kiss; she smiles wide. "I have a great vibe from you. Let's get out of here," she says. We go back to her shop. As we enter the store, she turns the music on, putting the lights on low. There is a desk in her office where we go. She grabs me past the doorframe and passionately kisses me while unbuttoning my top and moving toward the desk. I start unzipping the back of her dress. We caress each other's breasts. I feel the tension release from my body, arousing me. I'm creaming my pants. I unclip her bra and start sucking on her erect nipples. Moaning in delight, I lick all the way to the top of her panties, then slip them off. I caress her beautiful bald pussy and rub her in circular motions. She begins giggling. I take a finger and stick it into her while I rub her clit with my thumb. Moaning louder now, I feel the heat in her body. She's very wet, and so am I. I move my tongue across her thighs. Her juices smell and feel like sweet nectar. Feeling the energy in my body, I know I'm going to climax soon. I want her to climax too. I thrust two fingers deeply into her pussy, moving them forward and backward to reach her sweet spot, causing pulsing inside of her. She's quivering now. I feel my pulse rising. We are both climaxing. Her orgasm is all over my hand. I'm shaking now as I gasp, my juices all over my pants.

Resting

❖❖❖

Lying beside you while you sleep, I listen to the rhythm of your breathing. Softly you snore. I touch my breasts, caressing them, gently squeezing them. I lick my lips, tasting how lush they are. My nipples become erect, standing up as if I'm cold. But I'm just starting to warm up. I squeeze them harder and pinch my erect nipples. Arousing my senses, I smell my essence in the air. This causes me to feel the rush between my legs. The rhythm of your heart next to my ear makes me become wet. Moving my hands to my pussy, I massage her gently. Her juices are flowing; she wants you to wake up and lick her. Arising out of your rest, you kiss me passionately, sucking my tongue with your firm, soft lips. I am dripping wet now as I feel the sexual energy between us. I rub my pussy more vigorously now, stimulating her to bloom. You start licking and kissing my inner thighs. I moan gleefully. Now you are licking my clit in circular motions. She responds with swelling and my essence. My heart rate is up, and I feel the vibrations in my pussy. She is ever so hot and swollen, juices flowing like water. Moaning loudly now, my whole body starts to quiver. I hold back. I want the climax to last. You lick me from top to bottom, circling my butthole and thrusting your tongue deeply into me. I squirm with elation, breathing heavy. The hotness of your tongue flicking my clit is euphoria. This is it. I'm climaxing as my pussy pulsates deep inside. With a gasp, I release. My body shakes, and my essence spills into your mouth. I love our morning routine.

Raining

~~~ ❖❖❖ ~~~

We are together at my house fooling around in the living room. Outside, it is gently raining. You are so erect. I'm so wet. We are passionately kissing completely naked. The smell of my essence fills the room as I rub my pussy and you watch. I grab you and lead you outside to the backyard, the rain caressing our skin like little kisses. You go down on me as I sit in the lawn chair. Slowly you lick my pussy, teasing me with your tongue, making her swollen and hot. You flick my clit vigorously with your tongue, causing me to quiver under the coolness of the rain and the arousal of my clit. I want you so bad deep inside of my pussy. As you are rising, you slip your erect cock into me, thrusting deeply as I slide on the chair. We are laughing and panting with each thrust. This is erotic, and my pussy is responding by flowing with juices. I feel the pulsating of your cock as my body temperature rises. There is no turning back. I'm shaking with desire as the rain splashes down, sizzling on my skin as you thrust into me. The heat between you and me is pure energy. You feel it too as you moan enthusiastically while you rhythmically pound my pussy. We are both close to climax as the rain falls like fire between us. My pussy is vibrating, and I'm shaking from the extremes of warmth and coolness. I gasp as you climax, and I feel the gush of your ejaculation. Our juices flow together and run out of me like the rain flowing down my legs. We get up and run back in the house, giggling and laughing with euphoria.

Puppy Love

~~ ❖❖❖ ~~

I'm playing in the park with my dog. A beautiful older lady approaches me. "What breed of dog is he?" she asks.

"A Siberian husky purebred," I reply.

"Wow! Is he friendly?" she asks.

"Only with women," I say with a wink.

"Oh, that's awesome. I like dogs too. I don't have any because I work all the time and don't have the time to care properly for one," she says, winking back. I have a beautiful fit body that the lady is obviously staring at. "How do you stay in shape?" she asks.

"Walking my dog everyday and the gym," I reply. Liking what she sees, she invites me to her place to chat about my dog. We arrive at her house, which is very modern. There is clean modern furniture all around the house with lots of modern sculptures and art. We chat in the kitchen, my dog lying at my feet. She's wearing a sports bra and leggings. Her supple breasts show that her nipples are hard. I'm getting wet just admiring her physique. She has so luscious round hips and perky breasts.

"I love your smile," she says, "and you have the most succulent lips. I just want to kiss them."

"Which set?" I ask.

"Both!" she says, laughing. We laugh and start kissing passionately, sucking and nibbling on each other's lips. Her breasts feel so soft in my hands. I slip her out of her bra and start sucking her nipples. She starts rubbing my clit through my leggings. I'm getting so wet.

"I want to taste you," she says. I slip off my leggings, and she goes down on me. I giggle with euphoria. She presses her dominance deeply into me, thrusting forward to ignite my urges. I want to climax, but I hold off because I want it to last. Breathing heavier now, I'm moaning.

"You taste like honeysuckle," she says. "I can't get enough of you." I'm playing with my nipples, arousing all my senses. I can smell her hair mint shampoo and feel the warmth of her breath against my pussy. I feel the moisture of her tongue as I become juicier and juicier.

"I want to taste your land of milk and honey," she says. Moaning more loudly, I feel the heat and surge between my legs. My entire body is quivering; my pulse is racing. She licks me vigorously, and with a gasp, I release. My pussy lips pulse. My juices flow in her mouth as she gulps it all up.

Pleasure

❖❖❖

You're standing in the corner of the bedroom holding your hard cock. You are stroking as you watch me masturbating on the bed. I'm moaning enthusiastically, making my pussy wet. She comes to me, caressing my hair with long strokes, licking my lips as I lick hers back. Licking your lips, you stroke your cock more vigorously. You are like a shadow in the room. She and I start kissing passionately, sucking each other's tongue with loud moaning. My hands move to her delicious breasts, caressing and squeezing gently. She reaches for my pussy and feels I'm wet. At her rubbing my clit, I wiggle my hips into her soft, firm hand. I feel the blood rushing to my pussy. Her rubbing in circular motions over the top of my clit makes my pussy lips swell, and my juices flow. Slowly she moves to my pussy with her mouth, running her tongue from my lips down my chin, neck, and chest. I feel the moisture and warmth of her tongue as she licks my skin. As she reaches my pussy, her hot breath on my pussy causes me to quiver with anticipation of what's next. Then her warm, wet tongue flicks my clit vigorously. This causes my pulse to race as I feel my heart beating faster. Rhythmically my hips wiggle up and down at her licking. I grab my breasts and start firmly caressing them, gently pinching my nipples. I'm going to climax. As my pussy quivers, the pulsating inside me feels like euphoria. I close my eyes. My breathing is heavier. Beads of sweat form all over my skin. With a gasp, I exhale and release all my juices into her mouth. Watching all of this, you grin and shake as you ejaculate your essence all over her ass. We all sigh with relief, hugging as we come down to earth.

Online Fantasy

I'm an online fantasy girl. I leave my home to allow the maid to do her thing. When I arrive back, I see the house still in disarray. I follow the sound of moaning to my bedroom. Much to my surprise, my maid is sprawling on my bed using my props. It's intriguing to watch her. I feel like one of my viewers. Watching her is turning me on. An idea comes to me: I'll join her. I ask her if I can video us together. She smiles and timidly says sure. I set up my ring light while she tidies the room. Lying together in all my lingerie, we look stunning. We start kissing affectively. I sense her shyness. Using my tongue, I lick her lips, moving down her chin to her neck. There, I suck and lick feverishly, causing her to squeal. Relaxing, she seduces my breasts, cupping them with both her hands. I reach over to feel her breasts, making her nipples erect. She pulls back a little, and I smell her perfume lingering in the air. My senses are overwhelming me. I feel her tension and hesitation. This arouses me more. I want to please her. I reach for her pussy, which is surprisingly wet. I seduce her pussy lips with rubbing. Her moans tell me she is releasing herself to me. After removing her thong, I feel her pussy is swelling and dripping wet. My own pussy is wet and vibrating. I go down on her with all I have in me to seduce her to climax. I enthusiastically tongue her clitoris. She tastes ever so sweet like caramel. She's moaning louder now, rhythmically grinding her hips in my face. The vibrating inside of me is intensifying; my pulse is racing. The feed from my fans is blowing up; they love this as do I. Her smell and taste are more than I can endure. She is perspiring and quivering as she grinds my tongue. All of a sudden, the gush of her essence flows down my face. My fans cheer! I climax with a squirt, and we laugh at the elation.

Olympics

⋙ ❖❖❖ ⋘

As I watch the summer Olympics on television with my wife, a beautiful gymnast is swinging from the uneven bars. My wife has an athletic body like the gymnast's. I just love her figure. I blush, and my wife notices. My wife leisurely kisses me with a passionate caress of my breasts. I lean over and undo her top. I caress her supple breasts, twisting and pinching her nipples gently. A passion erupts between us feverishly; we take each other's clothes off. I feel the wetness between her legs, making my heart race. She's moaning rhythmically to the sounds of the music coming from the television. I feel her hands caressing my breasts, squeezing firmly, making my nipples erect. I feel for her bald pussy, which is dripping wet. I stick my finger in to make her quiver. Kissing her mouth, I suck on her tongue as I finger her. She moans louder now. I feel the pulse in her pussy. I am wet, my juices flowing. All my senses are heightened. I can smell her perfume. I hear the moaning and hum of the television. I rub her vigorously on the clit, making sure she is truly juicy. As her juices flow over my hand, I reach for the toy box. I pull out the dildo and slip it into her. Giggling, she grabs my hair, pulling it up. Moving the dildo slowly in and out of her, I feel my heart beating faster. I want to make her climax. She starts to shake, thrusting her groin into the dildo, moaning gleefully. I'm biting my lip watching her, then I shove my tongue deeply into her mouth. I feel the perspiration forming on my brow. She is going to climax. I want her to. I want to taste her. I'm in euphoria. Pulling out the dildo, I go down on her. She's so delicious like honey and jojoba. We are both breathing heavy now. Her body is quivering, and she gasps. Her juicy spirit flows all over my face. I exhale and feel the pulsing in my own pussy.

Older Woman

❖❖❖

The doctor walks in the office. She's the most beautiful woman I've ever met. She's wearing a short skirt and blouse. I am so grateful I am the hire out of all the candidates for reception. Her long hair flows breezy around her as she walks. I am so much younger than her. She has her life together while I'm still figuring mine out. It arouses me how professional she is. I just want to seduce her. She tells me she likes my outfit today. I smile shyly, nodding as I say thank you with a giggle. She smiles and winking says, "Lunchtime meeting in the exam room."

At lunch, I enter the exam room, stating, "Lunch tacos anyone?" I am giggling.

She reaches for me, pulling me close, passionately staring in my eyes. "You are so beautiful," she says as she tenderly kisses me. I feel the soft wetness of her lips against mine, the taste of her coffee, the smell of her perfume. I know it's going to happen. I welcome the sexual advances because she turns me on so much. Undoing my dress, letting it fall to the floor, she caresses my breasts over my lace bra. She squeezes and rubs the top of my nipples. I feel my nipples becoming erect. The warmth of her hands on my breasts makes my heart beat faster. The surge of passion goes to my groin as my pussy becomes wet. I reach for the buttons on her blouse, undoing them slowly to expose her perky breasts. I start sucking on them feverishly, licking the nipples and squeezing them with my hand. Her moaning only excites me more, my pussy flowing like water, running down my thong. Leading her to the exam table, I put her in the stirrups. I see she is wet through her thong. I lick her thighs she wiggles and moans. In circular motions, I lick her clit, tasting her essence. I stick my tongue into her pussy. She rocks her hips and clit over my tongue, all the while moaning louder. I'm starting to cream myself. I know she is going to climax soon; her pussy is swollen and pulsing. I use my fingers and plunge them deep inside her pussy while I lick her from top to bottom. She is breathing heavy, and perspiration is forming on her body. She smells like summer rain. Her neatly manicured pussy is dripping and quivering as she gasps and climaxes into my mouth and hand. She's gasping, but I don't stop as she moans uncontrollably. She yelps and squirts as I climax down my leg.

Nude Beach

~~~ ❖❖❖ ~~~

As I'm lying on the nude beach in my area, I'm playing with my toys. My vibrator is humming rhythmically as I pleasure myself. I'm biting my lip as the vibrator massages my pussy. Licking my lips now, I start to moan. This all feels so good. Warm sun kissing my skin, cool breeze filling my nose with fresh air, the sounds of waves caressing the beach all add to the euphoria. Then out of the corner of my eye, I see him standing there behind the rocks, stroking his erect cock. My eyes widen as I wave for him to come over. Smiling respectfully, he moves toward me. Kneeling down beside me, he touches my breasts, timidly caressing them gently. I moan louder now. This is so arousing. My pussy is all wet and juicy. He leans in and starts sucking, kissing, and licking my breasts while he strokes his cock vigorously. I see how hard he is, and he has a little drip right at the opening of his penis. My pulse rises. My pussy is quivering inside. I want his hard cock to penetrate me aggressively. Seeing I'm super wet, he moves down on me, running his cool tongue from my supple breasts toward my pussy. As he licks my clit slowly, I feel elation. I want to climax. He gently kisses my inner thigh, then thrusts his hard cock inside of me. He vigorously rides me, and I feel the tightening in my pussy. I'm going to climax. I'm breathing heavy and moaning enthusiastically. I gasp, and the juices flow over his hard cock. As my pussy opens up, I exhale, satisfied. He pulls out. I taste his sweet juices, and he exhales loudly with a gasp as he falls beside my body. We kiss and hug, giggling at the ecstasy of the previous moment.

Naughty Work Play

~~~ ❖❖❖ ~~~

I walk into the law office every morning. She's sitting behind her desk. I'm taken aback with a rush of heat to my groin every time I see her. She's so beautiful with her flowing hair and big eyes. I bite my lip. I wonder if she knows how much she turns me on. I smile and say good morning.

"Good morning," she replies with a smile. "I will see you in the conference room later," she adds with a wink.

Later in the conference room, we meet. She's wearing her glasses, a skirt, and a blazer. She knows I like to watch her play at work, so she brings out her vibrator and sits on the conference table. Pulling her close, I unbutton her blouse. These luscious breasts pop out. Cupping them with my hands, I begin sucking on them. Giggling excitedly, she turns on the vibrator. I unzip her skirt. It falls to the floor, exposing her garter and stockings. My pulse rises as the heat between my legs heightens. I'm becoming wet. I want to watch her play. She runs the vibrator over her lace garter and between her legs. The rapid buzzing over her thong is making her wet.

"Show me your delicious breasts," she says. I remove my sweater, exposing my pink bra over my succulent breasts. Staring at my breasts, she rubs the vibrator over her pussy, moaning rhythmically. I caress my breasts as the vibrator hums, arousing all my senses. I smell her perfume and the scent of her juicy pussy mingle in the air. I feel the rhythm in her moaning and the hum with the vibrator. My juices are flowing. My slacks are wet. I want to climax but not yet. I see how wet she is becoming. Her moaning is louder now.

"I'm coming," she gasps. Her body quivers, and she squirts all over the table. I cream my slacks. We smile at each other and kiss gently, bringing each other back from the euphoria.

Morning Coffee

— ❖❖❖ —

I'm in the kitchen wearing my black lace thong and bra while making your morning coffee, adding a little holiday cheer. I come to you lying in bed, delivering your coffee with a smirk and a wink. You grab me, kissing me intensely on the mouth. I shove my tongue down your throat as we giggle. Putting the coffee aside, you flip me on the bed and start stimulating my inner thigh with your tongue. You lick my pussy seductively while you tease her occasionally, flicking your tongue over my clit. Giggling gleefully, I feel my pussy twitch as her juices start to flow. Slowly now you lick my clit in circles with just the tip of your tongue. My pussy swells in response to the simulation. I'm breathing in deep long breaths. As I moan, you nibble on my clit. I feel my nipples are hard. Clutching my breasts with both my hands, I caress them, feeling the lace against my skin. Moaning, I rock my hips into your tongue vigorously. Now you lick me, grabbing my hips with both your hands. You take my thong off with your teeth. I feel your enthusiasm. As you thrust your tongue in and out of my pussy, I feel the pulsing inside of me. Beads of perspiration are forming on my skin. I see him watching, and this excites me more. He's vigorously stroking his cock. You thrust your fingers inside of me deeply, reaching for the front of my clit. The pulsing inside of my pussy feels like euphoria. I want to climax. Biting my lip, I hold back, thinking not yet. I want this to be epic. He's sweating now; he's going to climax too. You massage my sweet spot. I gasp. Feeling my heart race, I exhale slowly, trying to hold the feeling. Yelping loudly, I squirt all over your hand and his face. He shoots his spirit in sexual climax all over my body.

Mermaid

⋯ ❖❖❖ ⋯

The sun is setting. In the twilight, there is a shadow. I pause and adjust my eyes. Her figure appears slick and slim as she forms out of the water. As the night sky starts to show her beauty, the moon is coming out full. The starry hosts twinkle down, illuminating the sand. As she walks directly toward me, I feel my heart beat faster, keeping rhythm with the waves as they hit the sand. She is fully naked, a scrumptious beauty curvy in all the right places. I feel the coolness of the ocean air as it touches my skin, the warmth of the day settling away. I'm becoming wet as I lick my lips to fully take in this beauty. I reach out and touch her on the face, caressing her cheek with my hand. She turns and kisses my hand erotically, licking my palm seductively. The heat of her tongue and wetness of her mouth entice me. I feel the tingling in my pussy; it's becoming juicy. She pushes me down to the sand and kisses me frantically from my mouth to my navel. My supple breasts are awakening, and I grab them sensually. I play with my hard nipples as she works her way toward my pussy, flicking her tongue over my pubic bone. She is driving me crazy with excitement, making the pulsing in my pussy more intense. I taste the air; it's salty. I lick my lips and moan. She tickles my pussy with her tongue tip, sending spasms through me. The energy I feel is fulfilling. I'm going to climax. She's sucking the life force out of me. I know I'm never going to be the same. My juices are flowing like the water now. She sucks it all up. Inside my pussy is quivering, then he arrives. With a deep thrust, he enters me, his throbbing cock touching my very soul. I yell for release as he penetrates me. My pussy is completely surrendering. With a deep thrust, he gasps, and I feel his ejaculation flow into me. Rising, they leave and swim back to the ocean together. I'm lying shaking on the beach, wondering if this is real or fantasy.

Massage

At my spa appointment, I tell my masseuse, "Please relieve my stress." She lays me down on the massage table. Her strong, supple hands begin rubbing and squeezing my neck firmly but gently. The tension and anxiety is melting away. I feel her start to kiss my neck from the back of my ear down to my shoulder. Her seductive lips arouse a tingling in me. My temperature is beginning to rise. The warmth of her tongue and breath against my skin causes the hair on my arms to rise. Moving down my body with her tongue, she stops at my luscious breasts. I feel the sensation of her wet mouth sucking and tongue licking my perky breasts. I hear the sucking sounds and feel the warmth happening in my pussy. I'm responding to her seduction. My pulse is rising; my pussy is becoming wet. I start moaning. While sucking and kissing my breasts, she reaches down to my pussy with her hands. Her firm, strong hands are rubbing my clit tenderly. My juices are flowing. I feel the quivering in my pussy lips. The sensual seduction is taking my body to a state of euphoria. I'm so relaxed now, feeling warm and loose. She runs her tongue down to my clit, licking slowly at first while penetrating me with strong, supple fingers, reaching upward toward my sweet spot. As she rubs from the inside and licks the outside, I know I'm going to climax soon. I take a deep breath, feeling the pulsing through my body. I start to shake. Gasping uncontrollably, I feel the surging rush in my body; it's ecstasy. Now I exhale, releasing all my tension. My pussy pulses. I'm climaxing. The juices flow like warm, wet water from me. I'm perspiring all over my body. The sweet smell of honeysuckle fills the air. She kisses my pussy and dries my body off, smiling at me.

Lawyer Appointment

— ❖❖❖ —

Arriving on time to my lawyer appointment, I notice there are no men in the office. A sensual, luscious woman receptionist leads me to a private room. As I wait in the room for my lawyer to show up, the receptionist starts to undress. She takes off her suit jacket, revealing a black bra through a see-through blouse. Then in walks the lawyer, a luscious woman in a dark-blue suit jacket, miniskirt, and heels. I feel my pulse rise. My blood is rushing to my groin. The lawyer smiles at me seductively and starts to stare at my crotch. The receptionist is smiling too. Taking off her glasses, the lawyer leans into me. My pulse rises. The receptionist undoes her blouse. The receptionist takes the lawyer's hand and turns her toward herself. They kiss passionately in front of me, caressing each other's breasts. I see the heat between them as they suck tongues with moans of delight. They undress each other to their bra and thong. I feel euphoric. My blood is racing through me as I stare in disbelief. The receptionist is sucking the lawyer's erect nipples. I hear their moans and passion between them. I undo my pants. My cock is pulsating with energy! I stroke it gently as I observe them. The lawyer runs her tongue down the receptionist's firm stomach, stopping at her belly button ring. There she circles with her tongue. The receptionist puts her hand to her pussy. I can see their thongs are wet. Their juices are flowing. I want a taste. I lean in to taste the lawyer's essence. She squeals excitedly. This makes me feel the surge of energy rushing to my tongue. I feel the warmth and the sweet juices like nectar. Arousing my senses, I smell her essence. She is like a flower in spring, fragrant and bright. We are all energizing each other with tickling sensations to our very souls. The moaning from them is like ecstasy to me. It is more than I can bear. I feel the warmth in my cock. The surge is happening in my balls. It's rushing out of me. I climax all over my hand. The lawyer's juicy pussy and the receptionist's moans enhance the experience.

Landlady

I'm a horny landlady. The first of every month, this hot young lad comes over. I'm going to surprise him wearing nothing but a black lace bra garter and thong with heels of course. I hear the knock at the door. I know it's him. I open the door. He's wearing short shorts and a tank top. He's carrying his gym bag. I'm in awe of his physical body. *I must have him,* I think to myself. His mouth drops at seeing me. I know he likes what he sees because his groin starts to bulge. He's here to pay his rent. I place my hand on his crotch and invite him in to count his rent money. I close the door and lead him to the dining room, which has my huge solid oak table and chairs. He sits on the dining room table. I pull down his shorts and gaze in amazement at his scrumptious shaft. Grabbing with both hands, I stroke it aggressively, licking and kissing the head. Turning, he lifts me onto the table and starts grabbing my breasts and caressing them passionately. I feel my heart rate rise, and I moan enthusiastically. We are sucking face. He nibbles on my bottom lip, then runs his tongue down my neck. Arousing all my senses, he pinches and twists my now-erect nipples. I'm breathing deeply now. As he runs his tongue over my chest and past my belly button, I feel a surge in my pussy; she's responding with wetness and swelling. He starts licking and kissing my inner thighs, causing a rush through my body as I start to quiver. He slips his tongue inside of my pussy, moving in circular motions. My juicy pussy pulses with excitement. I moan loudly now as he continually sucks and licks my pussy. He massages my flower with his tongue. I want to scream. I want to climax. He stands up and deeply thrusts his shaft in my pussy. She pulsates around his enormous membrane. He rides my pussy rhythmically. I squeal and exhale deeply. I explode all over his beautiful membrane. He pulls out as I suck his essence up in my mouth.

Ice Spa

~ ❖❖❖ ~

You invite me to a cold-water dip spa. I had never heard of that before. You tell me it is super great for you. The latest thing, you say. I think, *Yeah, I'm into new experiences.* We arrive early and change into our bikini. Inside the sauna, we watch each other perspire. I see the beads of sweat form on your brow. I smell the faint odor of your body wash, arousing me. After sitting in the heat for awhile, we start to kiss. I run my fingers over the beads of sweat between your breasts. You suck my tongue vigorously. I feel faint from the emotional overload. My pussy is wet inside and out as my pulse rises. We moan rhythmically with each other as we embrace bodies. Being too sweaty, we climb into the icy cold water tub. The extreme cold against our hot skin makes our nipples completely erect. We gasp. I feel the rush of heat just between my legs. I play with your hard nipples, twisting and pinching them. You squeal gleefully and passionately kiss me as you gently rub my pussy. I'm moaning, feeling joyful as my pussy blossoms. Despite the cold, you feel how hot my pussy is, her juices flowing over your fingers. You pull aside my bikini bottom and thrust your finger in me. As you enthusiastically push your finger forward and backward to arouse me, I'm breathing heavy now in short gasps. I reach down and feel how warm and juicy your pussy is. We sit in the icy cold water rubbing each other's hot, wet pussy, moaning and exhaling heavily. We want to climax together. We suck each other's tongue with desire in our hearts while we vigorously rub each other's hot, juicy pussy. This arouses the sensations of pulsing deep inside our bodies. With a deep breath, we gasp and climax together, allowing our pussy to squirt into the icy water, creating a warm current over each other's hand.

Home Early

❖ ❖ ❖

I come home early from work. I open the door slowly to surprise you. I notice you are not there. I hear a slight humming noise coming from the bedroom. Following the sound, I observe you through the partially open door. You are in fantasy play wearing a naughty maid outfit. Enthusiastically on all fours on the bed, you are passionately sucking your favorite dildo with your saliva flowing from your mouth. You are moaning while your favorite vibrator pulses on your pussy. I can see you are wet by the glistening of your thong as you massage your pussy vigorously. This is all very arousing for me. My penis is erect, so I drop my pants and start stroking it gently, bringing forth my early juices. You are moaning louder now. I observe that your pussy is swollen as you rhythmically rock the vibrator while you suck the dildo. Hearing you moan, seeing your juicy pussy, I feel I want you. I open the door fully and stand behind you. I smell your essence in the air, so I slip my hard cock into your juicy swollen pussy. We fit together like a glove on a hand. Gasping for air, you choke on the dildo in your mouth. I push deeper inside your quivering pussy, holding you as I thrust in deeply. You squirt all over my hard cock. With loving surprise, you look at me and climax again. I turn you over, spreading your legs open. I begin kissing and licking all the juices from your hot swollen pussy. Your body shaking and breathing heavy, you embrace my shaft. I moan as you stroke my hard cock vigorously in both hands while licking up my early juices off the head. Excitedly you take your dildo, thrusting it deep inside you while you seduce my shaft. I see perspiration forming all over your body. You are moaning delightfully. This makes me feel like a god. My cock is pulsing in this euphoria. We are both about to climax. You yelp as I pull out and shoot my essence all over your breasts. We kiss and hold each other all afternoon.

Home Alone

⋯ ❖❖❖ ⋯

I am home alone lying naked on the sofa, feeling horny, so I start playing with myself. As I gently caress my breasts and lick my lips, I moan with excitement. I reach for my vibrator and start it up; it hums to life. Rubbing it over my face then down my neck feels wonderful as the vibrations arouse me. My pussy is becoming wet with anticipation. I move the vibrator to my breasts, making my nipples erect from the stimulation and cool air around them. I moan softly with delight, thinking, *I want more.* I move the vibrator to my thighs, teasing my pussy by running it up and down my inner legs. My pussy is juicy flowing like a river. I tease my clit some more as it vibrates over the top. I moan and giggle. My body quivers, the cool air touching my warm skin and the vibrations on my clit. I imagine you here sucking on my breasts and kissing my lips seductively. I might climax, but I hold off. I want to really enjoy this moment. As I rub my clit more with my vibrator, I feel my pussy lips swell and the pulse arise inside of me. It comes in waves as the vibrator massages my clit. My juicy essence fills the air, making a sweet aroma. Breathing deeply now, all my senses are alive. I smell sex in the air. I hear the soft music I am playing in the background. I taste the cherry lip balm I have on my lips. My heart is pulsing through my body. With every beat, I'm closer to climax. I gasp at the air in front of my face. I can't hold off. The vibrating waves inside of my pussy consume me. I climax with a deep breath.

Groceries

∽ ❖❖❖ ∽

I'm at the grocery store doing my chores. In walks a biker who doesn't remove his helmet. I head to the cereal aisle and notice that he is following me. His tight jeans and obvious upper-body strength excite me. I feel my heart race, thinking to myself, *Is he following me?* I head down the seafood aisle; there he is again. I see the water boil in the fish tanks. The lobster is cooking. I want to escape, but something is drawing me to him. I go over and touch his arm. He responds with a persuasive gesture by grabbing my breast. This is going to happen. I rip his top off and start licking and kissing his torso. His firm six-pack abs flex under my tongue. I'm wet like I've never been before. My juicy pussy is creaming my thong. I undo his buckle and pants. He is throbbing hard, standing erect before my face. I grab it with both hands and stroke it vigorously while licking the head. He tilts his head back and becomes loose, falling to the floor. I begin to devour his energy, taking in his very soul. My juices are flowing; my pussy is swollen. I lift up my skirt and mount him. Moaning loudly, I ride him feverishly like the wild woman that I am, my pussy pulsating. I'm going to climax. I feel the gush as my pussy explodes. As I push off him, he shoots into my eye. Everyone is gathered around with their mouths open. I hear over the intercom, "Clean up seafood aisle!"

Exam

❖❖❖

I arrive at my gynecologist appointment for my yearly check-in. I'm always nervous because she is so beautiful. I just want her to seduce me. The nurse calls my name and takes me to the exam room. I put on the gown and lie naked from the waist down on the exam table with my feet in the stirrups. She enters the room. I feel my pulse rising. The room has become very warm. Her lush breasts under her sheer blouse reveal she is wearing a black lace bra. I want her to examine me thoroughly. Her smile is warm and friendly, which makes me tingle. She sits down between my legs. I breathe deeply at her soft caressing of my inner thigh. This makes my juices start to flow. I think to myself, *Does she know how attracted to her I am?* I have a beautiful shaven pussy. She seems to be noticing because I feel her firm fingers rubbing me. My breathing is becoming heavy. I feel bliss. *She is going to thoroughly examine me,* I think as I smile. She uses her fingers to examine me, gently pushing them deep inside of my pussy, moving them from front to back until my pussy is vibrating and wet. I'm moaning now as she pushes firmly in me. Now with her tongue flicking up and down over my clit, I start to climax. My body is quivering, and goose bumps form on my skin. I feel the swelling of my pussy lips. How juicy I am as the wetness flows. I'm in ecstasy at this moment. I exhale deeply and yelp, biting down on my lip as I climax in her face. I think to myself, *Another yearly exam done.*

End of Shift

⧫⧫⧫

I'm waiting at the bar for you to finish work. It's loud and busy. I look across at you working, your beautiful physique muscles in all the right places. Your long hair is in braids the way I did for you before your shift. I love your arms and thighs. They are perfect in your uniform. You look so stunning. I just want to caress you all over with my tongue. You see me staring and smiling, so you come over. We go to our secret place by the mailboxes. You start kissing me passionately. I feel like I'm going to faint, caught up in your embrace. As you run your tongue over my neck, I'm feeling like a schoolgirl. I'm feeling a heat in my pussy as my pulse rises. You feel down between my legs, making my juices flow. My thong becomes wet from my juicy pussy. My heart is beating fast, causing my pussy to swell. I'm moaning rhythmically to the background beats coming from the bar. I know you are aroused by the swelling in your pants. I'm quivering now as you rub my pussy. I feel elation. Then in walks a beautiful woman with a fit body, smiling wide. She pulls down my thong and begins licking my inner thighs. You squeeze me tight so I don't fall. I'm dripping wet now; it's running down my leg. I'm in ecstasy. I want this moment to last. I breathe deeply. She sticks her tongue in and out of my pussy. I know now I'm going to climax. Your cock in your pants is pressing firm against me. I feel her hot moist breath on my clit. I yelp, and the gushing starts as I climax into her mouth. Then you unzip your pants and enter my pulsating pussy. Thrusting deeply, you deposit your power inside of me. We all giggle and hug tightly at the intense moment we just had together.

Drunk Love

I prepare for bed lying in my underwear. I drift off to quiet slumber with my headphones in, listening to my favorite beats. As my eyes close, I feel the sensual touch of hands gently caressing my body and feel the vibrations from the music. I imagine beautiful women rubbing oil all over my body. This arouses my senses. I feel the coolness of the air around me and the warmth of the hands seducing me. They massage my torso, focusing on my erect nipples. All of a sudden, I feel them licking my nipples. I feel my penis grow. I'm becoming fully erect. I tense, but their reassuring hands relax me. They move down my body, stroking my groin. I feel goose pimples rising on my skin. I smell the fragrance of roses in the air and the taste of honey on my lips. I anticipate their next move as their hands move toward my shaft. I'm here but not. The euphoria of it all feels like a dream. I feel the surge through my shaft as they stroke it gently. I feel the warmth of their hands and the pressure of their tight grip. This is engaging my mind. I feel the pulse through my body, a surge of energy. I release something; it's my juices. I feel the wetness on the tip of my shaft. They massage it around the tip. This sends spasms toward my heart, which is beating fast. I submit to the pleasure, feeling ecstasy in my veins. They stroke my shaft more vigorously as they feel the pulsating of my hard cock. Then I feel the wetness of a tongue licking the head of my penis. It's so tingly like little shocks going through my body. Then they devour my shaft in a mouth. I feel the wetness and the heat. It's more than I can bear. I explode at the sensation and release all of my essence over myself. This is something I will never forget—the sensation, the feeling, the euphoria.

He wore a tight skirt and a fluffy blouse. His makeup is perfect. His hair is very big. He has lush lips and lashes that went on forever. The bulge at his crotch entices me. Whatever is a girl supposed to do? I approach timidly and ask about his clothes. He smiles flamboyantly and tells me who his fashion designer is, intriguing me. I want to be as beautiful as him. I caress his arm over his long gloves. He turns and grins. I like what I see as I grip his succulent shoulder. He leans in, kissing me passionately. My heart flutters. He's sweeping me away. I must have him. We kiss, passing tongues feverishly. I'm becoming wet, arousing my senses. I feel the heat in the bar. I hear the music rhythmically thumping. There is nothing holding me back now. I'm all in. He's rubbing my breasts as I rub his crotch. He is fully hard and at my disposal. I rub vigorously. He moans. My core is juicy. We slide to the floor and grind each other. I lift his skirt and feel his enormous hardness. I'm sweating with anticipation as my pulse rises. I'm creaming my yoga pants. I feel the swell of my core as my energy surges there. He reaches down, grabbing my core aggressively. He is seducing my core with his strong fingers. I stroke his hardness, frantically wanting him to shoot his essence in my hand. I feel the tension in his hardness and the pulsing that it produces. He pushes his fingers in my core as I moan enthusiastically. I feel the vibration through my body as my inner pussy starts to climax. His juices are flowing as I massage the head of his member, rubbing his essence in. We exhale deeply and sigh with release as we hug.

Dancing

⋯ ❖❖❖ ⋯

As I am dancing in the club getting all hot and sweaty, he is grinding against me. I reach over and grab his long hair and seductively kiss his lips. My lips drip with excitement. I rub my groin against his leg, making me wet and juicy. I swing back, letting him observe my breasts popping out of my skintight dress. He reaches down and caresses my breast. I slap him across the face, forcing his next move. He grabs me and thrusts his tongue down my throat. The music slows. We leave the club and head to his restaurant. The place is closed, so we go to a booth. He undresses me like magic. I feel the bulge in this pants, thinking he is going to indulge me. He grabs my scrumptious breasts and, squeezing them tightly, starts to suck on my very core. After bending me over, he proceeds to lick my lotus flower, pulling my lace thong to the side. I moan uncontrollably. I feel my heart flutter. Vigorously his force flicks my flower. I'm spasming now, shaking all over, my flower dripping and vibrating. He pulls out his erection and takes me from behind, exhibiting his strength with each thrust. We fit together like a glove. I can feel the pulse in his erection. We grind as we moan enthusiastically. Time passes quickly. As I feel the surge to climax, I hold off, wanting the climax to be elating. He thrusts deeply, making me yelp. I'm in euphoria. The orgasm is lasting. I feel my pussy throbbing. He yells as he shoots himself into me. I release my pussy. Everything opens up, and the fluids run out. Wide eyed, he smiles, and we hold each other for awhile, all the juices flowing down my leg. He leans in and sucks up the essence, making me shiver with joy.

Dancing in the Rain

We are playing in the rain. It's rolling over our dresses and bodies like splashes of joy. We are swinging around in complete bliss. I notice your breasts as your dress starts to cling to your body, showing off your scrumptious figure of curves in all the right places. She has supple breasts, small waist, and lush hips. Smiling, I pull you closer to me. We hug and kiss passionately, indulging each other's lips sensually. Your soft, supple lips arouse all my senses. I feel my heartbeat rise. I feel for your pussy and notice you have no thong on. I rub you gently, and you respond by becoming juicy. You moan quietly and undo my dress. The refreshing cool rain dances on our skin like soft kisses. You start twisting and pinching my erect nipples. Now the juices of my pussy are flowing. Using my power over you, I push my fingers deeply into you with circular motions to entice your flower to bloom. You gasp in ecstasy. As I push harder inside of you, I feel your vibrations. You start to squirm and wiggle, moving your hips rhythmically on my fingers. You are moaning louder now. I rub your bean with my thumb vigorously. I'm so wet. I feel the warm gush rolling down my legs. You are breathing heavy and panting. Your pussy is expanding and contracting. You are climaxing. I feel your essence flow all over my hand as I cream my thong. We are giggling in euphoria as the rain splashes over us, relieving the heat and passion from the moment before.

Cool Shower

— ❖❖❖ —

As I shower with cool water running all over my body, I start thinking of you. I run my hands over my body. Feeling my breasts, I think how you gently caress my nipples and suck on them. They become hard with arousal. I can smell your shower gel. Thinking of you is so exciting, your beautiful body and supple bosom. Your tight ass and lush breasts! I enjoy the way your tongue licks my pussy. Like you are making love to her. I move my hands down to my pussy with thoughts of you. I stick my finger in and out. I moan softly. Lathering soap all over my body, the slippery suds release the feeling of euphoria. I love the smell of your shower gel. It makes me feel close to you. I take a deep breath and gently caress my nipples, making them erect. Playing with them, I imagine you are here. I feel the heat in my groin. I know my juices will run. I run my hand down to seduce my pussy, thinking it's your hand on me. I close my eyes and breathe excitingly. I rub my jelly bean vigorously. She is becoming swollen. I know I'm wet as the juices flow from my pussy. I feel the warmth run down my thighs as I stand in the cool shower. I grab the showerhead and turn it to pulse, putting the head between my legs. With the cool water pulsating and my finger rubbing together on my jelly bean, I feel the rush of my climax as I gasp slightly. Inside my pussy is expanding and contracting. I yell your name, squirting juices all over. I smile to myself. I love fantasizing about us together in the shower.

Cheers

We meet at a bar, both drinking beers. I am the most beautiful woman you have seen. I have been thinking of our date all day. I wear my purple suit jacket and skirt with a black lace bra and thong. We dance, and my jacket pulls open to expose my bra and supple breasts. You grab me by the pussy and pull me close. All the men are staring. We kiss passionately, tongue to tongue. Everyone is turned on. We leave as you take my hand, leading the way. Inside the washroom stall, you pull off my jacket, feverishly caressing my breasts as we suck each other's tongue. Your sensual taste of whiskey excites me. Grabbing your crotch, I feel you. How ready to bloom you are by the bulge in my hand. My breathing intensifies into heavy gasps. You undress me with your teeth. The sensation of the cool air in the washroom caresses my skin, giving me a shiver. I feel a heat coming over me as my pulse heightens. I massage your crotch passionately, and I become wet between my legs as all my energy rushes there. I'm anticipating what's next. You lift me against the wall. I'm quivering with delight. Slowly you lick me, teasing my clit with little flicks of your tongue. My breathing is rapid while you slurp and penetrate me enthusiastically with your tongue. I'm moaning loudly now. I know I'm going to climax. I am still stroking your membrane, and you gasp for air. My pussy pulsates. Her juices are flowing freely from her. I want to climax. You are close too because I feel the throbbing in your groin. As I climax with a yell, my essence flows directly in your mouth. We stand freely now. There is a wet spot in the crotch of your pants. Laughing with each other, we kiss passionately while your pants dry.

Bubble Bath

⋯ ❖❖❖ ⋯

I decide to take a bubble bath because you just left for work. I climb in the warm bubble bath to soak in the tub, sliding down under the water. I come up, touching my face sensually. Licking my lips, I feel how supple they are. I like my lips; they are soft and firm. I am a good kisser I think as I lick my lips again. I move my hands down my neck, rubbing firmly with the soapy water. I feel the smoothness of my skin. This is arousing my senses. I smell the fragrance of the bubble bath as it lingers in the air. I feel the warmth of the water surrounding me in the tub. Slowly sliding my hands over my breasts, I caress them joyfully. They are slippery and soft. I feel sexy now. I continue to gently squeeze my slippery breasts, making my nipples erect. My nipples poke out of the water to the surrounding cool air. I play with them, twisting and pinching them, gently arousing my inner woman. This makes me feel the heat between my legs, rising as the energy surges through me. I rub my foot up and down my smooth, sexy, shapely legs. I moan quietly as I play with myself. I move my hands to my pussy; she is becoming swollen. Rubbing her in gentle, rhythmic circular motions, I moan louder. I feel tingling bubbles floating over the top of my bean and the pulsating deep inside of myself. I'm so close to climax. I grab my dildo with objective. It feels so good like a hard membrane seducing my inner me. I'm breathing heavy. With the vibrations of my pussy, the quivering of my body, I yelp; and the gush of my soul flows out of me into the warm water. The feeling of euphoria surrounds me. I'm at peace.

Biker

❖❖❖

I flip through the television channels because I'm bored. I look at my husband and give him puppy eyes with a smile. Licking my lips, I invite him to come with me to the new strip club. He nods and smiles, grabbing his keys. Outside the strip club, he pulls me close and passionately kisses me. I'm mush in his arms. I feel my heart race. Inside the dancer is on the stage. I lick my lips and take a table with my husband. I watch her swing on the pole. She has a strong, fit body. I find this arousing. I feel warm all over. As I take off my jean jacket, my husband notices my erect nipples. Smiling at each other, we kiss passionately, sucking each other's tongue. This is making me wet and him hard. Then in walks a biker still in her helmet, her curves showing through her leather outfit. She walks right over to us and takes my hand, leading to the private rooms in the back. Following closely, my husband is curious as to what is happening. In the private room, she unzips her outfit. Out pop scrumptious breasts. I play with them by caressing and squeezing them. She never takes off her helmet but starts taking off my dress, exposing my bra and thong. I'm juicy now. I look at my husband, and I see that he is playing with himself, pants at his knees. The biker caresses my breasts with her perfectly manicured hands. I moan in elation. She reaches down, feeling my pussy, warm, wet, and pulsating. Nodding, she sticks her fingers inside while her thumb massages my bean. Mouth open, my husband is stroking his cock vigorously. I feel the pulsing inside me. I feel she's wet and hot. Her fingers feel like ecstasy to my core. I know I'm going to climax soon. Breathing in ragged, heavy breaths, I feel my body quivering. This is euphoria. Watching closely, my husband is going to climax too. I lean over and start to seduce him with the delicious heat of my mouth. She thrusts her fingers with force deeply inside of me. I gasp in slow pants, climaxing all over her hand. She pulls her fingers out and puts them in my husband's mouth. He climaxes. I devour his essence. We never see her face behind the helmet. Then just as quickly as she came in, she leaves.

Backyard Party

I am playing my guitar in the backyard with my neighbors. We are all singing and laughing together. They start to dance, rhythmically rubbing their bodies together in a very sensual way. This is arousing me. I feel the warmth cradling between my legs as the sun and cool breeze caress my skin. He embraces her passionately, and they suck each other's tongue. I feel my heart race. I'm getting wet at the weight of his desires. As my juices flow, I observe him undoing her blouse; her perky breasts pop out. I cannot take my eyes off her. As he squeezes her breasts, I think that I want to be doing that. She starts moaning. My pussy is dripping wet. I put down my guitar and cut in on their dancing. He grabs my groin under my dress, feeling my juicy thong. He smiles and puts my hand to her breasts. I immediately caress them by twisting and pinching her erect nipples. We start kissing and rubbing bodies together. She moans softly. He is rock hard as he presses his cock into her back. I reach down to feel her flower. She's not wearing any panties. I rub her clit gently in circular motions right on the top. He's breathing hard and rubbing his crotch. She pulls me to the grass. Her flower is so juicy. I seduce her pussy slowly with my tongue circling her clit. She moans louder as he unzips his pants. I am juicy tasting her essence. I seduce her from top to bottom, thrusting my tongue deep inside her pussy. She gasps and starts to quiver, perspiration forming ever so slightly over her skin. He's stroking himself, breathing in long inhales and exhales as he makes his dick instinctively come to life. With her arousing moans, I feel the pulsating in my vagina. I know I will soon climax. She starts rocking her pussy over my mouth, rubbing my tongue vigorously over her clit. Her swollen pussy is flowing juices like water as she shakes and pants at her climax. I devour all her juices up as I climax. He pours his essence on her breasts as we all take a deep breath.

Around the City

We are on the streetcar snuggling up to each other because it's cold outside. Hugging each other closely, you turn to me smiling, licking your lips. We are thinking the same thing, so I wink at you. We get off the next stop and find a hotel room. Inside you unzip my jacket while pulling off my hat. Passionately you kiss me while I undo your jacket. You excite me by slipping your tongue into my mouth, which I seduce on feverishly. Now I'm pulling off your sweatshirt and your pants. You unclasp my black lace bra. My perfect round breasts pop out. You grab them with in such a way my head starts to spin. You lick my nipples, which tingle in anticipation. My nipples become erect at the warmth and sucking of your mouth. I smell your cologne, arousing my senses. I feel the blood rushing through my body. I'm blooming at the sensual sensations of your strength. I feel your force flow through me. You remove my pants. I am excitedly into this. I know you are too because you are rock solid hard. You lay me back on the bed with my legs in the air and caress the inner me with your firm, soft hand. I feel my pulse rising. My core is on fire; her juices are flowing. I feel your hot, moist tongue licking my thighs. I squirm rhythmically to your touch, moving my hips side to side, following you in a manner of speaking. Taking your fingers, you force and thrust them into me with circular motions, causing my fluids to run like water all over you. You pull them out of me and put them in my mouth to keep me from gasping. Moaning, I think to myself, *I taste so sweet.* You lick my pussy from bottom to top. The sensation of euphoria is coming over my entire body. I'm quivering. I feel the surge in my pussy as she squeezes and relaxes; she's pulsating now. I feel you mount me slowly and deeply. I'm climaxing. My body is shaking. My core is pulsating in waves. I gasp at the sensation. We climax together, collapsing into each other's arms.

Apartment Hunting

I am looking for an apartment with my girlfriend. She's the most beautiful woman in the world to me. Her soft lips that kiss so tenderly are so exciting to kiss. We are looking at a fully furnished unit today. We go in with the office manager to view the unit. He tells us to look around because he has something else to attend to and leaves us there. When we check out the bedroom, there is a queen bed beautifully made. I grab her in my arms and hug her tightly. She giggles. We are thinking the same thing, to give the bed a try. She unbuttons my blouse, exposing my supple, firm breasts. She caresses them affectionately. The warmth of her smooth, soft hands squeezing my breast causes my pulse to race. I feel the heat rising between my legs. This woman is everything to me. I pull off her top and unfasten her lace bra. She's so exciting, her fit body. Lying on the bed, we are kissing and sucking each other's tongue, tasting our coffee breath from this morning. I slip my tongue into her mouth as she moans. I feel my pussy is juicy. Reaching down, I feel hers is too. We slip out of our slacks, and I begin rubbing her wet flower. Her thong is dripping. I have her juices flowing, and she's breathing and panting. I am now creaming my thong. I think she is so hot, and I want to taste her. I slip off her thong, devouring her flower until it blooms. She responds with wiggles and thrusting her hips into my face. Using my fingers, I slip deep inside her. With two fingers, I burst open deep inside her with vigor toward the front of her flower. Now I vigorously lick on her clit, her body quivering and perspiring. Inside her pussy, my fingers feel the pulsing and juices running. She's going to climax soon! She gasps, and her body shakes. I feel her pussy tighten up around my fingers. She exhales, then the release. Her vagina opens up with a flow of her warm essence. I lick her pussy again as I climax, tasting her very soul.

Alter Ego

❖❖❖

I'm a gay man trapped in a woman's body. I dress in trousers and dress shirts always. Once I fall into a deep sleep, I fade to my alter ego. He's a strong muscular man with a brush cut. I feel the sensations of warmth consuming my body. I hear the trickle of rain outside my window. I smell the cologne I wear. I feel the touch of his hands as they seduce me. Burly hands with thick fingers massage my torso, arousing my inner desires. My penis is becoming erect. I know this is going to be euphoric. He runs his hands down my body, paying special attention to my erect nipples on my pecks. Slowly he moves to my cock, stroking it gently, gripping the head. I am perspiring in the anticipation of his tongue. Then I feel it, a quick flick over the top of my cock. A wet and moist tongue tickles me. My cock tenses and hardens to the sensation. The burly hands vigorously stroke now as his tongue licks my head. I feel the sting in my balls start. The whole mouth is engulfing my shaft now. I feel the teeth and tongue together as they devour me. The sensation in my balls is growing, rising from deep inside of me. I reach down and scratch my balls as he slurps on me more vigorously. I'm biting my lip as the tingling in my balls ignites. I lick my lips as he deep-throats me. The sensation is too strong. My essence is sliding up out of me. I am no longer in control. The surge comes, and I spread my ejaculation everywhere, then drift deeply into sleep.

All Tied Up

~~~ ❖❖❖ ~~~

It's late in the evening. The shadows are forming on the walls as the sunlight fades behind the horizon. She comes to me in her corset bra and thong. She kisses me passionately, caressing my breasts by squeezing and rubbing them. I'm submissive to her as she gently lays me down on the bed and ties my hands to the four corners with ribbons. You're watching in amazement, smiling. I'm aware of everything—her soft lips against mine, the taste of her warm mouth, the smell of the wine on her breath. You stroke your cock gently, producing precum. She moves to sit on my face. Her juicy pussy fits my mouth like a puzzle piece. I lick slowly, teasing her. She's moaning enthusiastically as she rocks her hips over my tongue. She arouses my senses. I feel the heat rising in the room as my flower becomes wet. You observe, smiling a grin of anticipation, your fist tight under the head of your cock. Her pussy is blossoming as I seduce her from back to front. She's climaxing into my mouth. She reaches down to my juicy pussy and, rubbing in circular motions, causes my flower to bloom. The sweet taste of her juices flowing into my mouth is like an aphrodisiac. I'm perspiring and quivering at the sensation. I'm going to climax. My swollen pussy is pulsating. You bend down and start to feverishly seduce my pussy. Your cock is fully erect and throbbing. I climax with a gush flowing into your mouth. My flower is blooming and vibrating as you thrust your cock deep inside of me, deeply penetrating as I shake beneath both of them. I'm in euphoria as you cover me with your essence deeply inside.

www.ingramcontent.com/pod-product-compliance
Lightning Source LLC
Chambersburg PA
CBHW032207040426
42449CB00005B/471